WINGS OF RED

Original Poetry

Krista Maguire

KRISTA MAGUIRE

In Loving Memory of Lindsay Carole Bell

28.08.1968 - 01.03.2012

The cover image of the poppy was painted by Lindsay while receiving day therapy at St Ann's Hospice in Little Hulton, Salford.

Death is not the end

WINGS OF RED

Petals of red spread out like wings
The souls of the dead reach out and sing
We hear their voices we heed their call
'Remember us for we did fall'

The blood the sweat and the tears
The courage hiding all their fears
Marching to a future they would not see
Yet they did it for you and did it for me

The footsteps taken can be traced
To a troubled time and a painful place
Where the ultimate sacrifice was made
Now in the ground their bones are laid

On battlefields where blood was shed
These flowers grow crimson red
Upon the graves of the young and old
The echoes of the past unfold

This beautiful bloom is a constant reminder
To treat others better treat others kinder
To live a life of humility
To forge ahead with integrity

The eleventh day and the eleventh hour
We wear with pride the poppy flower
Paying homage and showing respect
Always remembering lest we forget

MOTHER NATURE

She's your best friend and your worst enemy
Building a day around her is what we do normally
We check on her regular or the day before
To see what she has planned what she has in store
Her actions definitely speak louder than words
She affects everything from the bees to the birds
Her hands touch us all with warmth and with ice
She's not always lovely and she's not always nice
Her breath reminds us of her strength and power
Her tears which fall can flood rivers in an hour
Her icy fingers can freeze all in her path
Her smile can warm us and make us all laugh
She cradles this place which we call home
Dishing out the weather from Beijing to Rome
The protector of all things which we take for granted
From the natural world and the one we have planted
The manageress of the soil we walk upon
Of the life we all share beneath the rays of the sun
Reaching all the four corners of this beautiful earth
You know whom I speak of and you know of her worth

MAKE MY DAY

The sound of nature and life in general
Bring peace to the heart and soul
From living things to rocks and minerals
And from the north and the southern pole

Early morning and between day and night
Is when you can find yourself relaxed and calm
No matter where you are at this time
It's a break from life's funny farm

A moment and place to sit and think
Or maybe just to clear the mind
To recharge and energize
What will this new day find

There will always be a reason to smile
And many reasons to cry
Constant questions we will ask
Though we may never get the answer to 'why'

So hark to the sounds of nature
They are there if you just sit and listen
Doesn't matter if it's a concrete jungle
Sweet melodies of birds will make your eyes glisten

And so a positive outlook is always a must
No matter what stands in your way
Get up get ready get your freak on
And go make somebody else's day

THE POWER INSIDE

Confused perplexed and misunderstood
When relationships break down it doesn't feel good
Words explode and chaos wins
Let us not be accountable for our fathers sins

The evil men do should not overpower
The love which prevails like a bloom of a flower
Deception and outrage like a cloak can shroud
All which is beautiful in a dark cloud

Push the deeds which cause strife to the side
Like the devil incarnate it often tells lies
Fervently relinquish and salvage the truth
Don't do an eye for eye or a tooth for a tooth

For that is falling foul to all which is bad
And will only leave you feeling bitter and sad
Dig deep my friend and find the strength to overthrow
Take this power with you wherever you go

THE DUST BUNNY

I heard a screech from my daughters room
'Intruder' I thought so I grabbed my broom
Up the stairs two at a time maybe three
'Mum mum come and help me.'

Into her bedroom I did burst
Thinking the complete and utter worst
Crouched on her bed and eyes wide
She pointed down 'that's where it hides'

Slowly slowly I dropped to each knee
And pulled back the duvet guess what I see
The most enormous fluffy dust bunny
Staring vehemently back at me

For those who have never seen one of these
They are neglected dust particles and can make you sneeze
Lint, hair and neglected debris
All these combined make the perfect dust bunny

I thought for a second and smiled a wry smile
The dirty beggar hadn't cleaned for a while
So I let out a howl and grabbed that fluffy bunny
I could hear her shriek and it was ever so funny

I dangled the intruder over her head
She screamed even louder and her face went red
'It's a dust bunny you messy little git'
What do you expect living in this cesspit!

This type of bunny is a pet like no other

KRISTA MAGUIRE

'Now will you please just listen to your mother
The moral of this story is simple dear daughter
Clean up after yourself you know that you oughta'

THE SLEEPY SHRINE

In the sweet surrender of the night
When the day is done and so is the light
The land of nod beckons to us all
And into sleep we gently fall

Warriors of the dark start to purge
The dream walkers do emerge
Where everything is slightly mad
And events occur both good and bad

Down the rabbit hole we drop
Behind the white rabbit with a hoppity hop
Vivid colors in mixed up places
And oddly some alien looking faces

There's no concept of time down here
And everything which we hold dear
Dwells alongside the dead
Continuing life inside our head

And when we wake from our sleep
We sometimes have a little weep
It's hard to leave loved ones behind
In dreamland they stay the sleepy shrine

BEHIND THE MASK

There's not a flaw on her face
Her makeup is well applied
And any signs of blemishes
Well they must have gone to hide
Hair is never out of place
Whether up or down
A frame encircles her gorgeous face
Her head would suit a crown
The clothes worn ooze money
Stylish and serene
With skin dipped in honey
She always looks pristine
Yet behind the mask of makeup
Beneath the expensive attire
Resides a woman so insecure
Who's life is rather dire
For it's all a front you see
It covers up the pain and sorrow
Yet she will rise and create herself
As she faces each new tomorrow
So don't judge the cover of a book
For appearances can be deceiving
Open it up and take a look
Understand what you're perceiving

THOSE DAYS

Memories of other times return
And my heart feels the yearn
For the days of the past
Don't they go by very fast

I know how to live in the present
And yes it's wonderful and it's pleasant
Yet to go back in time for one day
To be a child to laugh and play

I recall how Sundays were so long
Go to church to sing a song
Say prayers then back home
Outside all day the streets we'd roam

Names called at three o'clock
Could hear me mum from round the block
And smell the roast hmmm yummy
Big waist hug for my mummy

No worries no bills to stress about
My clothes on my bed all laid out
Each day much like the others
Toy fights with my sisters and brothers

Blissfully unaware of the struggle
To pay the rent or get in a muddle
Now I know what it's like
To scrimp and save for that bike

Yet those were the days my friend

KRISTA MAGUIRE

And yes we thought they'd never end
Of kiss chase and knock a door run
And slapped arse when we got done!

A jolt back to the here and now
A tender smile as I touch my brow
I've a house to clean but I'll visit again
To my wonderful past bottom of memory lane

JACK FROST

I can feel the presence of this man
It's in the bitter cold
And he will do all he can
As winter starts to unfold

He's the chill I feel when I shiver
The frozen ground below
And he makes me old joints quiver
As off to work he goes

He paints the landscape frosty white
With brushstrokes long and wide
And he works through the night
There's nowhere I can hide

He teases me with his artistic flare
Painting the skies above bright blue
But don't be deceived my friends
He's just tricking me and you

You know of this man I'm sure
And you know this is his game
For he visits once a year
And Jack Frost is his name

A NEW DAY

In the darkness of early morn
Hides a day waiting to be born
It fights against each shadow cast
Races against the clock so fast
Tapping gently upon the ground
Stealthily and without sound
It caresses buildings and tree tops
A moving halo it never stops
Until at last it beats the night
And covers earth with fresh new light
A new dawn a brand new day
To embrace come what may

THE LEGACY

Death is a journey to be taken alone
Flesh and blood gone just leaving the bone
Like a lonely dancer pirouetting into the night
The spirit remains though the body is out of sight

Back into the Earth the physical descends
Yet the essence of life never ever ends
The echoes of yesterday linger in the today
Photos and trinkets are here to stay

Life is infinity it gets handed down
Like a king or a queen we pass on the crown
What is left for others is our legacy
It is in each blade of grass each flower and each tree

THE OLD MAN

The deep ravines cover the local terrain
Now and then a crack tapers off into a smaller narrower lane
Each groove creating ridges so deep it has scarred the landscape
And towards the bottom lies a hole much like an empty lake
Further up two pools of lucid bluey gray stand adjacent
With just a hill separating them yet both rippling in unison
The water holes once bright with life lie sad and empty
Once abundant with tales of glory days aplenty
The years have not been kind to this once lovely gentle face
Weather beaten the youthfulness has left nothing not a trace

THE MONSTER

In the light there are shadows
Which dance upon the wall
There will always be darkness
When dusk comes to call

And as the clock ticks away
It's journey towards dawn
Every nook and every cranny
Provides a shape or form

A flash of light from a passing car
Can conjure up a waving beast
And the fear inside builds up
As it's arms stretch out and reach

It's not real it's not real it's not real
And I slam shut my eyes
For in those darkest of hours
The shadows tell their scary lies

THE UNDERGROWTH

There is a place full of trees
Where strange creatures dwell
Get down on your hands and knees
And follow the earthy smell
Push away the undergrowth
Move the leaves and the twigs
And you will start to see
The beetles and earwigs
Spiders of every shape and size
Scramble back into the shade
And other tiny little beasts
All which God above has made
The slugs and the snails
Moving really really slow
Leaving behind their trails
Everywhere they go
Then there are butterflies
Fluttering here and there
Ants marching in singles lines
Going who knows where
It's a world within a world
Of peculiar crazy bugs
Be sure to check them out
When you go walking in the woods

WHY WAIT

It's a funny old world
don't you think.
We are here for a while
and gone in a blink.
Through the rain fall
I still marvel at the world.
I sit at my window
and watch life unfurl.
The plants and the trees
the grass and flowers.
And people watching
I could do that for hours.
There's so much around
to be grateful for.
Even amidst grief
or the sadness of war.
Life and death the two
most certain aspects of life.
So cherish your husband
cuddle your wife.
Grab those close
who you love and adore.
Don't sit on your laurels
no not anymore.
Today is here so
make it great.
For tomorrow is not promised
So why would you wait?

MEMORIES

Sundays and Station Road is heaving
In and out of the crowd I'm weaving.
Match day and we sit on the wall
Trying to catch sight of the ball.
Suddenly we hear an almighty roar
The sound of the crowd leaves us in awe.
Oh how we loved those 'lovely' days
Soaked in the sun and rippled with haze.

Market day and what a sight to behold
Swarms of us everywhere both young and old.
Through the roof shoots rays of light
Stalls full of wonder and delight.
The fish at the front, chicken at the back
A naughty kid getting the odd smack.
Progress stores, our little Toys R Us
Market day, busy and all of a buzz.

Six week holidays that lasted forever
All out on the street no matter what the weather.
Making mud pies, playing Kick can
Blowing raspberries at the odd drunk man.
Mums and dads sat out in the street
Us jumping around with nowt on our feet.
Running home when we hear our names
Starving and dirty from playing make believe games.

Teenage life was hard but great
Always bloody grounded for getting in late.

Bethal Hall at seven fifteen
That's where I was when I was a teen.
First taste of ale and being sick
Falling everywhere and looking like a d-ck.
The Wishing Well and the top road
Who needed Town when we had our own.

A SNIPPET OF 76

It was a long hot summer and I was nine years old
One of the longest heat waves on record I'm told
You could fry an egg on the hot bricks
Back in the summer of seventy six

The school holidays went on forever
In the glorious sweltering scorching weather
Every day at four it would shower
Then streets would steam up and be dry in an hour

My mum would make a million ice lollies
Then sit with the neighbors under the shade of their brollies
Wafting their fans and still drinking hot tea
And in the heat which always seemed silly to me

Along came the famous dreaded water drought
Actually started in seventy five and ran throughout
I remember the ladybirds they were everywhere
On our clothes and even in our hair

When bedtime came there was no respite
The heat continued right through the night
Sleeping in only our knickers and vests
No need for the housecoat or the nightdress

Ah we had so many long days
All wrapped up in a hot summer haze
Popping tar bubbles and making mud pies
Yep that was my summer seen through my own eyes

THE BLADE OF A KNIFE

This is the story of a woman's life
One cut short by the blade of a knife
She met her beloved on a hot summer's day
He wooed her beguiled her in every single way
Flowers and gifts and promises were made
Yet at the same time mind games were played
The accusations became more and more
Your a bitch a slag and a dirty little whore
Social engagements became a thing of the past
For her bruises she couldn't always mask
He convinced her that she was ugly and fat
That he could get better at the drop of a hat
And in between all this mental and physical pain
He told her she was mad that she was insane
It all came too much for this woman to bear
She had to escape from this living nightmare
And on a hot summer's day much like their first date
Overwhelmed with despair and heavy with hate
She took a knife and plunged it into his heart
The one which broke hers right from the start
Now she lives in a different kind of hell
Cut off from the world in a cold prison cell
Even from the grave still controlling her life
One cut short by the blade of a knife

SHADOWS

Shadows stretch out across the land
Reaching outwards like a giant hand
Ever shrinking and ever growing
Like a river always flowing
It travels slow when it moves
Spreads itself into each groove
And as the light begins to fade
The world vanishes in the shade
Muted stillness is how it feels
And tiny details become concealed
Light and dark need one another
As if a sister to a brother
During the day and at a certain time
Shadow and light become entwined
It is at that time they become one
Though not for long and then the moment is gone

IN HELL

The hunger is profound
As it eats away your soul
Going round and round
Creating a deep dark hole

A nibble here a nibble there
Enough to start you off
What is this torrent of abuse
It's something you just can't scoff

It wears you down inside
Weighing heavy deep within
And that my darling dearest
That is how it does begin

Once it's crawled inside your mind
It makes itself right at home
Leaving all logic behind
Here comes the twilight zone

Rational thoughts are no more
Anxiety does take its place
Closed is every door
And now it's time to race

You try to outrun it
Scream and shout and yell
Sometimes you are triumphant
Not too long down there in hell

HAPPY HALLOWE'EN

What foul creatures will stir tonight
To give us chills and fill us with fright
These angelic children of the day
Will dress to chase the evils away
Witches monsters ghosts and ghouls
Zombies vampires there are no rules
Though none can call upon our homes
I hope on Facebook they will roam
And I know it's not for everyone
Please understand it's just for fun
So children beasts of the night
Fill yours hearts with spooky delight

HAPPINESS

You can find it almost everywhere
In the big things and the small
It brings a smile to your face
Indeed it could be over nothing at all
You can see it in the sky at night
In the morning just as day breaks
It can be located anywhere
Mountains valleys beaches lakes
You can locate it in your own home
As you relax with a cup of tea
Or chatting on the telephone
With your friends and family
You can come across it accidentally
Or choose to see it without trying
It really helps when feeling low
And it even comes when crying
You can feel it when it happens
It envelopes your heart and your brain
It can be affected by the weather
In sunshine wind and rain
You can share it with another
It's good to pass it about
Mother sister father brother
It can make you sing and shout
You can have it if you want it
It's there for you and me
I'm talking about happiness
Just smile and you will see

WHEN I'M GONE

Remember me after I have gone
Think of all the happy times
Turn your face towards the sun
For I will leave you signs

The orchards and the tall trees
And sweeping fields of green
Sugars floating in the breeze
Oh what a wondrous scene

Leaves which rustle like the sea
Sweeping out towards the sky
Don't ponder on the fact I'm gone
No time wasted asking why

The butterflies and bumble bees
Which hum and flutter by
The birds singing in the trees
And the eagles flying high

Think of me when rain does fall
As the heavens open up
And I will surround you with my love
I will calm the storm in your teacup

See the children playing happily
Hear their squeals of delight
And I won't be too far away
Even though I'm out of sight

Remember me as you live on

Not with tears and endless sorrow
For our time on Earth is precious
And we are not promised tomorrow

A NEW WORLD

Muffled and muted is the world
As snow drifts down upon it
Painting the landscape steadily
In a kind of beautiful white bonnet

The sky above appears lower now
As if heavier with the weight
And it falls without remorse
No blade of grass escapes its fate

And now it looks so other worldly
Patches of color here and there
No hint of human life as yet
No footprints anywhere

THE GATE

The weather beaten garden gate swings to and fro
Creaking under its own weight
with nowhere to go
The people who have opened it have left their mark
Even the folk who have stumbled in from the dark
A garden gate is the portal to another place
One which can welcome and lend a warm embrace
The paint is now peeling it has seen better days
Scorch marks here and there from the sun's hot rays
And if you look closely you will see letters etched in the wood
The declaration of two people who had fallen in crazy love
Yes this old rickety gate will last for many more years
It has already seen much happiness and felt a thousand tears

MEMORY LANE

I can time travel did you know
I think of when and off I go
That's the beauty of the mind
A cassette player it can rewind

I go back to a time and a place
Where I find a familiar face
Or an event which can bring joy
And sometimes one which can destroy

The happy faces are the best
Just to see a loved one I feel blessed
Even so they can bring a tear
Especially if that person is no longer here

I can time travel did you know
Like the tides it ebbs and flows
Inside our mind and deep in our brain
You don't need a ticket to get to Memory Lane

BROKEN HEART

Reflections on a life which should have been
She ponders on a hapless dream
Beneath her feet so hot it burns
Her path with all its twisted turns
Leads her to this wasted state
Is this it is this her fate
She scrapes away at the past
Exposing love which did not last
Hands sore and raked in blood
She suddenly understood
To love is to know such pain
Would she ever feel it again
Her heel she turns and walks away
Tomorrow is another day
For her beloved now rests in peace
As the sunsets in the east

THE PRECIPICE

Standing on the precipice
Of something so majestic
It is something so spectacular
And is totally fantastic
It's a place between yesterday
And the tomorrow
It's the right here and the right now
And life with all its happiness and sorrow
So recognise what is important
Know that the present is exactly that
It's a gift to be unwrapped every day
And to this I tilt my hat
Standing on the precipice
Of all that is happening now
Never mind about why and what
Don't worry about who and how
Love and laugh and yes cry
Be sure to embrace all the good and bad
Lift your eyes to the sky
And make this the best day you've ever had.

DEAFENING IS THE SILENCE

Deafening is the silence
In this crowded room
Bordering on violence
Of impending doom

I seek some comfort
Beneath the cotton sheets
Some kind of solace
Just me and my heart beat

Fear of being alone
Panic does take over
For in the twilight zone
It's hard to run for cover

A slither of day breaks
And a sense of hope returns
My body and mind aches
For peace and love it yearns

GRAB LIFE

Sing dance hold your head up high
Your so amazing and do you know why
Come on now go look at your reflection
You are the epitome of perfection

You see my friends there's no specifications
Perfection is full of imperfections
The outer shell is not what defines me and you
It's what's in our souls it's in all that we do

Looks and youth may change over time
But getting older is not a crime
Your still full of life and have so much to give
So get out there grab your life and live

A NEW LIFE

I feel an inner peace
For those who have gone
As they leave this life
A new one has just begun
I know they're still around though
A different shape or form
Maybe in another dimension
They have been reborn
For life in essence is infinite
There is no end not ever
Just the vessel we occupy
Which we all have to sever
We are more than a body
Much more than flesh and blood
Our spirit is invincible
And we are all that is good
So when my time comes
To shed the physical being
I'll be somewhere amazing
And I'll be busy living

A RETURN TO INNOCENCE

Oh to be a child again
Life just about to begin
Eyes wide with imagination
To not know of any sin
The joy of finding a penny
For it would bring good luck
Of losing yourself in make believe
Or an Enid Blyton book
Not a care in the world
No bills to keep you awake at night
No worries or stress at all
Not a frown line in sight
You never knew your parents struggled
What to give you for your tea
It was always on the table though
Full bellies for you and me
Treats were just that a treat
At weekend on a Saturday night
A glass of pop crisps and mars bar
Much to our delight
The kids today won't know
The terror of the outside loo
When at night we had to go
With creepie crawlies to watch us poo
Oh to be a child again

To play out wild and free
To run the streets with friends
Maybe fall and scrape a knee
I can recall those days of innocence
As if it were only yesterday
When life seemed so much simpler
In every single way

KINDNESS

It seems we are seeking some kind of validation
For not everyone is satisfied being part of God's creation

Each word which we utter and every move we make
We know it will affect others and cause their paths to shake

Grudges need not be held forever in our hearts
For they are circumstantial and have played their parts

Yet as we stumble onwards to somewhere we know not
We hope that our existence here will never be forgot

So tread with respect let this be your policy
The footprints we leave behind will be our legacy

OUR HOME

Mesmerizing and magnificent
Is this Earth we call our home
So many wonders to behold
So many places we can roam

The brooks, streams and rivers
Like veins pulse around our planet
As if a huge beating heart
Placed strategically upon it

The mountains rise majestically
Gate keepers of valleys down below
Where nature is truly free to be
And animal life can thrive and grow

The magic of the plants and trees
The insects which procreate
See the seeds of life drift on a breeze
In an ever growing state

The sun shines with all its might
Casting shadows across the land
Providing us all with warmth and light
With its enormous outstretched hand

The hypnotic tides of the oceans
Influenced by the moon's pull
How powerful are these forces
Terrifyingly beautiful

LOCKDOWN LOVE

Their eyes met across the store
And all about them faded away
Just for a second there
Neither knew what to do or say

She swept her hair behind her ear
He fumbled with his hand
And both felt something new
They did not quite understand

They blinked back to reality
And both resumed their shopping
Though they met again on aisle three
Both their hearts a popping

She smiled at him he smiled back
No mask could disguise this
Both imagined what it would be like
If they could share a kiss

It's hard to get to know someone
When standing six feet apart
It's even harder in lockdown
How does one even start

So they went their separate ways
Yet return they would for sure
For where else could they meet again
Maybe next time on aisle four

SHATTERED DREAMS

I waited and I waited until the sun went down
The smile I started off with now a hapless frown
My dress I bought especially had a bit of muck about the cuffs
And my shiny brand new shoes were sporting brand new scuffs
I checked my phone a million times but nothing there for me
And as dusk grabbed hold of the day I knew it wasn't meant to be
I'm such a fool why did I even wait more than an hour
My hopes and dreams in that moment allbut turned to sour
No call no text no nothing from him as I double checked my phone
Who does this to another person leaves them waiting all alone
I turned my collar up high and began my journey back
An ambulance flashed past me fast I almost had a heart attack
When I got home I wept into my third glass of wine
No second chances for him that man had definitely crossed the line
Stop stop no more dwelling on this silly situation
I'll watch a funny film instead let's see what's on television
Just before I switched channel the news flashed up before my eyes
I recognised that photo it was my date to be to my surprise
And then I saw an ambulance situated just around the block
I recognised the buildings it was my corner shop
Could it be was it he and suddenly it became so clear
When I saw a battered bunch of flowers on the roadside very near
'Died at the scene' is all I heard over and over again!
Outside the heavens opened and suddenly down poured the rain
The broken hopes and dreams of mine now no longer mattered
As All his hopes and dreams lay in the road side shattered

SUMMERTIME SUN

Oh to feel the sun upon my face and sand between my toes
Thoughts of racing to the sea stripping off these winter clothes
I want to dip my body into waters cool and float up and down
And safely let the sun kiss my body a gentle golden brown

I long to walk barefoot and fancy free amongst rolling fields of green
And make chains of daisies and buttercups the best the world has ever seen
To stroll beneath the boughs of a million cherry blossom trees
And watch the petals as they float by on a soft warm breeze

Oh summer can't come soon enough and I can't wait to see
All the colors of the rainbow return upon every plant and tree
To catch a whiff of barbecues and music playing here and there
Of settling down with a beer in a comfy old deck chair

I want to see skies so blue with barely a cloud in sight
And sit out beneath the stars until the early morning light
Come on now Mr Bluesky I think winter is surely done
Now it's time to heat things up and send over the 'summertime sun!

IN SLEEP

In sleep the world does change
A different life I lead
Where all around me is strange
And yet the flesh still bleeds

Just like Alice in Wonderland
Down the rabbit hole I go
All by myself no helping hand
To take part in a weird tv show

My friends are there but not quite
Loved ones fade in and out
And my home is neither here nor there
All my furniture is moved about

Sometimes I'm me as I once was
Younger and more agile
Other dreams I'm not myself
An alternative me for a while

Many times I am a spectator
Part of the audience if you will
Observing the actions of others
From a mountaintop or hill

Life speeds up and slows down
And some scenes are terrifying
In many dreams the dead return
Somehow death defying

I walk amongst the ghosts

KRISTA MAGUIRE

Of those who have gone ahead
Sometimes they speak out loud
Or the words appear inside my head

There are times I don't want to leave
I want to stay there in that dimension
Where anything is possible
A world high above me in suspension

Yet time is of no consequence
Whilst I'm in the land of nod
And I sometimes wonder when I wake
Was that the hand of God

SAVE OUR PLANET

As Mother Nature blows away
The bag begins to move
Choreographed by the elements
It gets into its groove

Now and then it slumps dramatically
But doesn't stay down long
For as Mother Nature exhales
So it rises with her song

Soaring now into the sky
As if St Peter has called its name
It reaches up with its handles
Rippling like a flame

At last it returns to land
And Mother Nature beckons me
'Take this and recycle dear
Or it will end up in the sea.'

THE DREAM THIEF

At night when all is quiet and still
A strange being is on the prowl
It hides in the dark shadows
On its hideous face a scowl

The darkness is it's sanctuary
It feels safe in the shade
Waiting for the world to fall asleep
So it can begin it's raid

Slithering into the minds of many
It steals all our beautiful dreams
Replacing them with monsters
The stuff which makes us scream

It is neither man or woman
Nor any animal we recognise
It's tricks us and it teases
With its nasty little lies

This 'thing' cannot be trusted
It's both a giver and a taker
You know what I speak of
It is the 'nightmare maker.'

THE BUTTERFLY

Spare a thought for the butterfly
It's life is short and sweet
Each one looks so delicate
And most live only for a week

Some may breathe for just a day or two
Though some as long as a year
But the average lifespan is so very short
That these beauties do appear

They arrive on the tail of the summer sun
And languish amongst the flowers
I could lay down on the sweet green grass
And watch them fluttering for hours

Some say they are messengers
To comfort us when feeling sorrow
From loved ones up in heaven above
To give us hope for the tomorrow

WHISPERS OF THE PAST

Echoes of the past remain
In photographs stamped with stains
Newspaper clippings of yesterday
The World Wide Web of the day
And the memories of yesteryear
Return the past and bring it here
Pictures of a black and white world
On sepia paper with corners curled
Images of boys in pass me downs
Pants so baggy akin to clowns
Scuffed knees and dirty faces
With talking boots and undone laces
Little girls in gingham frocks
With matching ribbons and matching socks
Hula hoops and skipping ropes
Rolley poly down the slopes
The echoes of the past return
And sometimes I do yearn
For the play streets of my youth
Out on the roads and on the roof
Children playing so happily
Until mum called them in for tea
So treasure all your photographs
For they can make you cry and laugh
And there's so much we can learn

When whispers of the past return

THE WOODS

Not a whisper of a breeze
Standing here beneath the trees
Just the sound of the birds
As they cheep their chirpy words

Trees stand as if spellbound
And the stillness is all around
The guardians of the woods
Create shelter with leafy hoods

A place to come to clear the head
And lay down on the earthy bed
A sanctuary from the rat race
Nature's perfect peaceful place

ANOTHER DAY

Delicate and fragile is this thing called life
It can be severed in a heartbeat with one slip of a knife
The bitterness of all things negative can conjure up a theme
Of one's worst nightmare and wash away the dream
As if waves licking at the coast of all the things we hold dear
Fervently moving back and forth until some details disappear
What's left behind is fragmented and is hard to comprehend
If these pieces are put back together will it be foe or friend
And like grains of sand slipping through our fingers
It's difficult to hold on to and so not much lingers
Adapt and evolve is the only way to carry on
For sitting doing nothing will never get things done
Take the bitter and the sweet embrace what comes your way
For it simply means you live my friend, live for another day

TIME

What is 'time' but just a number
Invented by man if you will
It sneaks passed us as we slumber
I wish we had more time to kill
Our lives are ruled by the clock
Decisions and deadlines
We should pause and take stock
So we don't miss details or miss signs

What is time I ask you my friend
Just another man made...idea
And without it our lives will still end
So is 'time' something to fear
We are aware when it's day or night
The skies will always let us know
So do we really need 'time'
For like the tides we can see the ebb and flow

What is 'time' I ask each of you
Do we really need to live by the clock
For if life goes on after ours is done
Then surely it's just a load of crock
I guess we won't ever know
Now we are so wrapped up with 'time'
So on that note I have to go
I have an appointment at half nine

BEYOND

Beyond the realms of all we know
Where colors so vivid and brightly glow
Rainbows abundant a sight to behold
And at each end a pot of gold
A place of peace and solitude
No hunger here plenty of food
All types of life from ant to whale
No cash needed there is no sale

Beyond the realms of what we know
There is a place where we can go
All forms of God's creations live
And taking is replaced with give
The battles and the wars replaced
No more fighting to be faced
Just fields and meadows and water pure
An untold paradise never seen before

Beyond the realms of love and life
Resides a world bereft of strife
A space where all is safe and good
And the reason why is understood
It's a sanctuary for all living things
Two legs four legs, fins and wings
Where lives are yet to unfold
Stories waiting to be told

Memories of a life before
Locked away behind a door

KRISTA MAGUIRE

Yet the lessons learned not forgot
Of why where when and what

AS DAY BREAKS

As dawn approaches the world rubs its eyes
And sounds begin as the nighttime dies
In the distance a lone car hums on by
And birds chirp high in the sky
They chatter to each other overhead
Making plans as they feather their bed
A soft mist swirls round the trees
And kisses the ground on a gentle breeze
It gives the scene an otherworldly glow
And drifts across the landscape and stays really low
The hush interrupted as all life comes awake
And even ducks seem louder upon the once still lake
The hustle and bustle gets louder still
And rain spatters on the window sill
It's a great time to rise and see the day
Before the stampede gets underway
When most of us are still asleep
Before the rush of human feet

BLESSED ARE WE

Oh how wonderful life can be
Not just in the physical and all that we see
There are other senses that can be stirred
Things that are felt and sounds which are heard
The laughter of children on a warm day
Excited voices as they make believe play
Fresh bread oh how I love the smell
And ground coffee, love that as well
The green green grass under one's feet
Feeling grounded oh how utterly sweet
The ice cream van as it jingles it's way
Onto our streets each summer day
Blessed are we to witness the simple things
A bird overhead flapping its wings
The hum of the sacred bumble bee
Busy working away for you and for me
Listen to the wind and feel the gentle breeze
Watch the sway of the waving trees
Close your eyes, listen and feel
You don't have to see to know it's for real
Life and love and in all its wonder
Sounds of weather like rain and thunder
Every day just take it all in
Inhale the goodness and get busy living

THE TRAVELER

I've lived so many different lives and I can't recall them all
Yet I believe I once was a Queen and a King who walked so tall
I've flew above this planet earth as an eagle and a dove
And each one of my lives were full of wonder and so much love
I've walked across space and time in various shapes and forms
And in each role I've lived I've weathered tempestuous storms
Some short lived like the common fly some long and even infinity
Yet each one so appreciated and full of divinity
I've battled my way to today and the here and the now
Always questioning what why where when and how
Yet maybe there's no definitive reason why I'm this human being today
Perhaps it's just the journey which matters as I go along my way
So I'll leave you with this thought great thinkers of the universe so vast
Today is all that matters so live today as if it's your last

RAINFALL

Rain…what is this strange phenomenon
So delicate how does it even carry on
A tiny drop from the skies overhead
Surely it dries up before it lands on my head

Gently wafting down to land
Still in one piece as I stretch out my hand
Softly softly it falls to the ground
It covers everything sometimes without a sound

Persistent it can dance for hours
Teasing the grass and the thirsty flowers
Drip feeding the rivers and the seas
Cloaking the shrubs and tall trees

Fooling the world with its ninja moves
Slowly building up as it's gets into its groove
So vital for life and so diverse
Another wonder of the universe

NEW LIFE

My pulse races as I spy
Birds overhead in the sky
The sounds of a new day
Begin with life in every way

Even the low hum of cars
Leaving behind polluted scars
Exhaust fumes taint the air
Cannot stop life anywhere

And amidst the humdrum
Each new day is welcome
New beginnings new starts
Excited beatings of new hearts

Fresh plants and forest trees
Cleansing the air as we breathe
Always working and so should we
To maintain this harmony

Far and wide this phenomenon
Never ends just carries on
Represented by the figure eight
Is infinite and worth the wait

WILD HEARTS

Across the inky blue lakes
To the shores of green
Up towards the rock faces
Which in the sun do gleam

This land once home to mankind
Knee deep in history
Now only the ghosts remain
Their departure no mystery

They took and took from the earth
And failed to put back in
Blinded by greed and power
Was their deadly sin

The silence of this land today
Is all that now remains
Yet hope of new life can be seen
In flowers blooming on the planes

The age of man has now gone
It's time for new and fresh starts
And underneath the rain and sun
Sound the beating of wild hearts

LET'S FLY

The eyes of the innocent are deep and pure
For they know nothing of what has gone before
Pools of wonder staring up into our eyes
Beautifully naive and clear as summer skies

Filled with excitement and curiosity
And totally in awe of all which they see
I try and view the world like a child
Dance and sing and go a bit wild

We teach our children isn't that the norm
Yet I've learned so much since mine were born
They remind me to enjoy the little things
That we can still fly we don't need wings

LOVE

Oh how beautiful is true love
Hand made by the angels above
Delicate yet strong and true
Clear as skies and just as blue

Like freshwater it is so pure
Seeping love from every pore
So bespoke so taylor made
So majestically unafraid

Tender and so alluring
Confident and self assuring
Emitting rays of bright sun beams
Across bubbling brooks and babbling streams

It can scale hills and mountains high
Can lift the spirit with wings and fly
Swim in rivers and sail the seas
And drift so gently on a breeze

Be ready when love comes to call
Let it wash over like a waterfall
Open your heart and let love flow
Take it with you wherever you go

LINDSAY CAROLE BELL

28.08.1968 - 01.03.2012

Delicate traces left behind
To gently poke and tease the mind
A memory wave of yesteryear
Increasing in size as it gets near

The wave is always on the go
I feel it daily and I know
That on this day it does trigger
A tidal wave which does get bigger

And just when it is fit to burst
When I'm feeling at my worst
A waterfall of warmth and love
Descends on me from above

The subtle tones of a voice
A cause for all to rejoice
Soft and velvet to the ear
Of someone held so very dear

No card to give no presents too
No grave to tend today for you
Just the love and memories
Of my brilliant and lovely sis

MY LY FE LL

Printed in Great Britain
by Amazon